Ukulele!

Pentatonic Songs and
Activities for Young Beginners

Level 1

by Andrea Gaudette

Andrea Gaudette, M.M.Ed.
andreagaudettemusic.com

Ukulele!

Pentatonic Songs and Activities for Young Beginners Level 1

Andrea Gaudette, M.M.Ed

ISBN: 9798852072788
Imprint: Independently published

For Shay

Note to Teachers

Musical development is akin to language development. We learn how to make sense with sound by immersing ourselves in examples and then creatively experimenting with what we hear. Our mastery of verbal expression develops as we continually listen, interpret, symbolize and generate our own ideas. Musical literacy follows this same trajectory. As we learn new notes to play and read, we should also be given ample opportunities to create and notate our own ideas. In keeping with this developmental concept, *Ukulele!* provides young beginners with opportunities to explore music notation and creation in each chapter. The processes of creating, performing and responding in this method align with the 2014 U. S. National Core Standards in Music. The progression of understanding pentatonic scale pitches is inspired by the philosophy of Zoltán Kodály.

Children also learn through social interaction, play and repetition. 10 pieces in this book have accompanying games which provide students opportunities to reinforce musical knowledge in a fun way. These group games may be used as activators to introduce new musical concepts or to provide routines at the start and end of each lesson.

Young fingertips are sensitive and beginner ukulele players need time to build up protective callouses in the left hand. This primer focuses instead on right hand finger style technique while emphasizing reading and playing the pitches of the open strings.

It is recommended that students sing each song before learning how to play it on their ukuleles.

This book may be used in both classroom settings as well as private lessons. The games are ideal for groups of children in grades 1-3. (Some of the activities are geared toward the younger student, while others are best for those who are older.)

For sound files of the repertoire in this book, go to andreagaudettemusic.com.

Finger Style Technique

This method does not use a pick. Instead, each finger of the right hand gets its own string.

- The thumb strokes down to play the G string.
- The 1st finger (index) strokes up to play the C string.
- The 2nd finger (middle) strokes up to play the E string.
- The 3rd finger (ring) strokes up to play the A string.
- The pinkie touches the body of the ukulele and acts as an anchor to balance the hand.
- The body of the ukulele rests between the ribs and right arm.

Contents

For accompanying games, see p. 94.

Chapter 1

Getting Started

The Parts of a Flower

The Parts of a Note

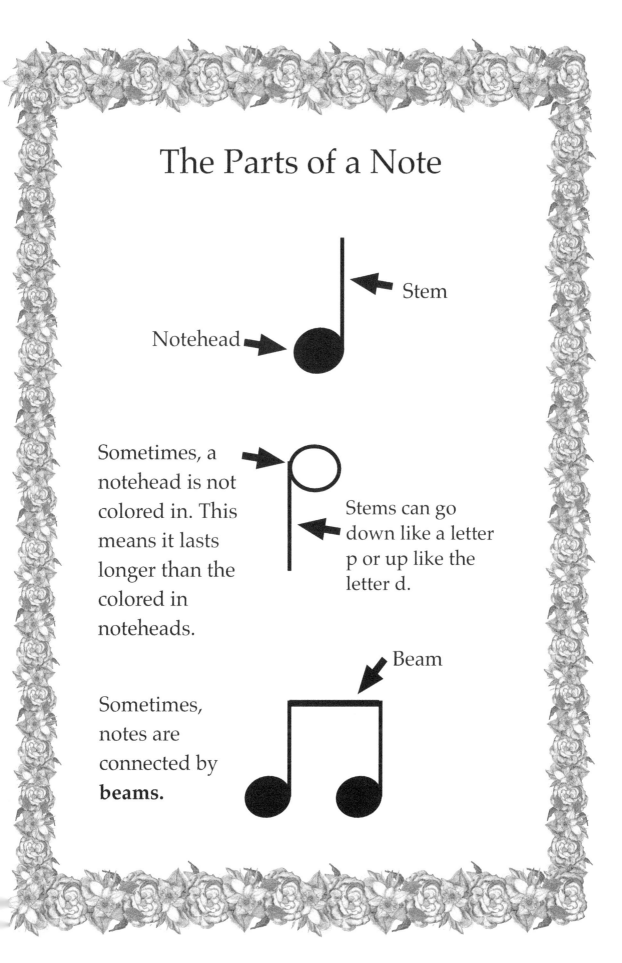

Stem

Notehead

Sometimes, a notehead is not colored in. This means it lasts longer than the colored in noteheads.

Stems can go down like a letter p or up like the letter d.

Beam

Sometimes, notes are connected by **beams.**

The Parts of a Ukulele

How many frets are
on your ukulele?

How many necks?

How many
strings?

How many tuning
pegs?

How many
sound holes?

The musical staff has 5 lines.

These birds are sitting on the lines, but their tails
are below the lines.

There are 4 spaces between the lines.

These birds are in the spaces between the lines.
Draw a bird in one of the spaces.

This is a note head. ○   This is a line note. ○

Notice how…

half of the head is above the line,

and

half of the head is below the line,

but

the head never touches any other lines.

This is a **staff**.

It has 5 lines.

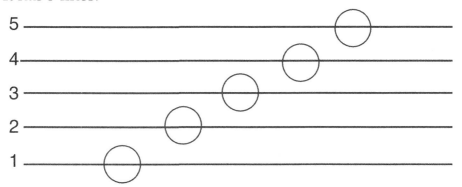

Draw one line note on each line.

5 ———————————————

4 ———————————————

3 ———————————————

2 ———————————————

1 ———————————————

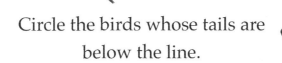

Circle the birds whose tails are
below the line.

Chapter 2

G and E

This is G. It sits on the 2nd line. G is the string closest to your heart. Pluck G with your thumb.

Draw 3 line note G's.

Draw some birds sitting on the wires like
line notes. Remember to put their tails
under the wire.

This is E. It sits on the 1st line. E is 2 strings after G.

Draw 3 line note E's. Pluck E with your middle (2nd) finger.

Good Night

Circle the E's.

American Folk Song

Good night, sleep tight,

see you in the morn - ing light!

When you master this song, go to p. 88.

Witch, Witch

Find the repeat signs.

Play the music in between
the repeat signs two times.

American Folk Song

Children:

Witch, witch fell in a ditch,

picked up a pen - ny and thought she was rich.

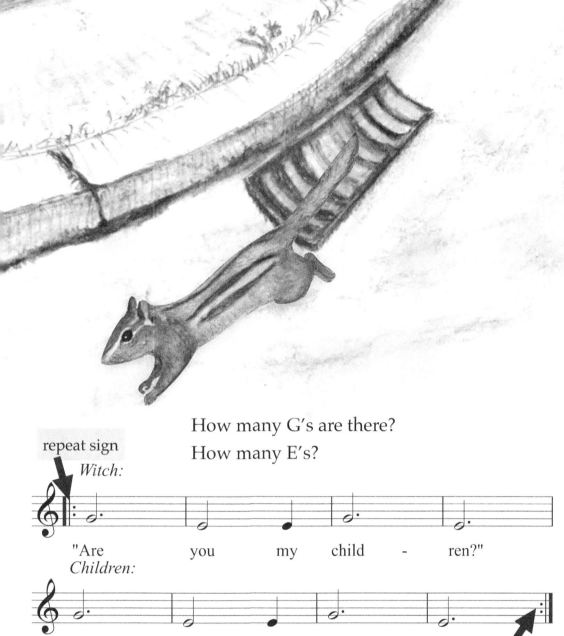

How many G's are there?
How many E's?

repeat sign

Witch:

"Are you my child - ren?"

Children:

Yes, we're your child - ren.

repeat sign

Witch:

"Are you my child - ren?"

Children: (Spoken) No, you old witch!

Draw the missing line notes.

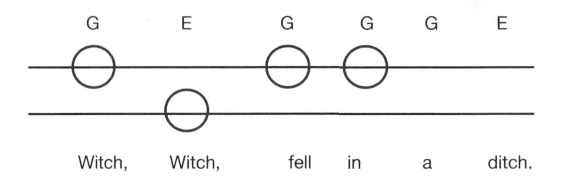

G	E	G	G	G	E

Witch,   Witch,   fell   in   a   ditch.

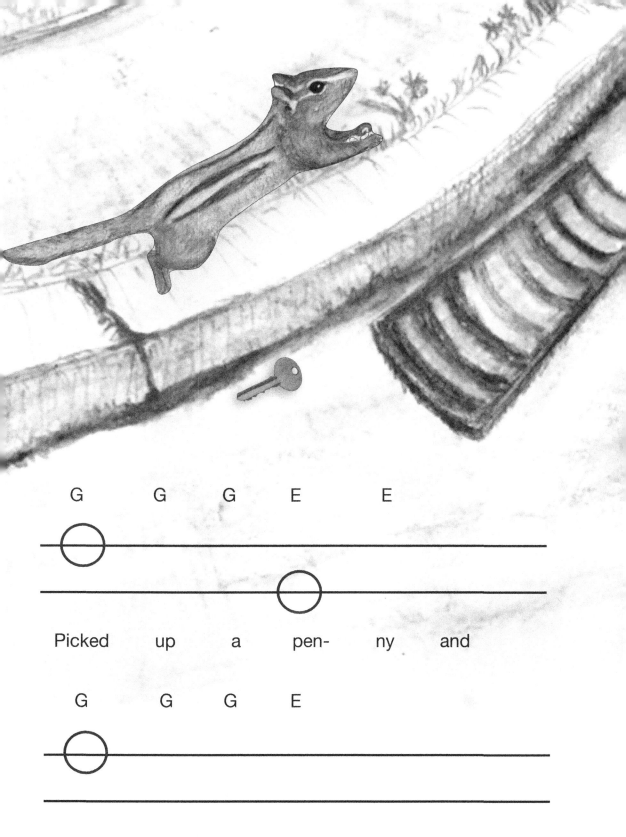

G   G   G   E   E

Picked   up   a   pen-   ny   and

G   G   G   E

Thought   she   was   rich.

Chapter 3

The Space Note A

Space Notes

This is a space note.   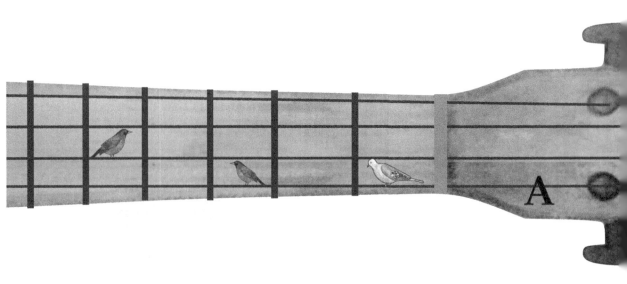   It sits in the space
between the lines.

Draw one space note in each space.

4

3

2

1   ◯

A is a space note that sits on the 2nd space of the staff. It is the string closest to your feet.

Draw 3 A's. Pluck A with your ring (3rd) finger.

Rain, Rain

Pluck A with
your ring finger.

American Folk Song

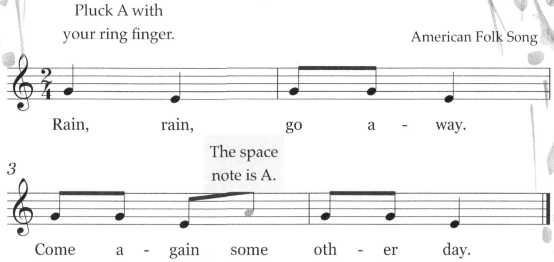

Rain,   rain,   go   a - way.

The space
note is A.

Come   a - gain   some   oth - er   day.

It's Raining

Circle the A's.

American Folk Song

It's rain - ing, it's pour - ing. The

old man is snor - ing.

This is a quarter note. Say "Town." "Town" has one sound.

 These are 2 eighth notes. Say "City." "City" has two sounds.

Say and clap the rhythm. Then strum* the rhythm on your ukulele.

♩	♫	♫	♩
town	city	city	town

* Strum the open strings. Stroke down with the backs of your fingernails, and up with the back of your thumbnail.

Fill the missing blanks in the chart. Say and clap the rhythm. Then strum the rhythm on your ukulele.

	♩	♫	
city			town

Fill in this chart to create your own rhythm. Say and clap your rhythm. Then strum the rhythm on your ukulele.

Lucy Locket

Circle the G's.

English Folk Song

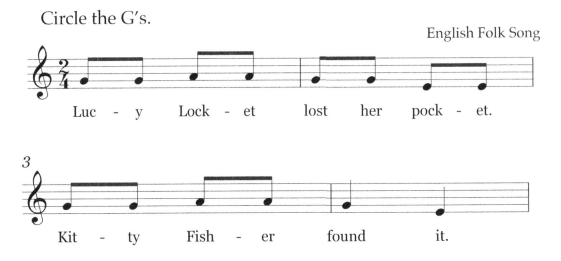

Luc - y Lock - et lost her pock - et.

Kit - ty Fish - er found it.

Are you using a different finger for each string?

Bar lines divide music into **measures**.

5

Not a pen - ny was there in it,

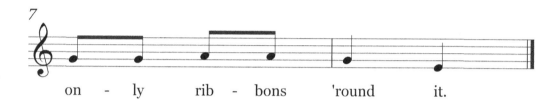

7

on - ly rib - bons 'round it.

How many measures are there?

How many **eighth notes** are in the first bar?

How many **quarter notes** are in the last bar?

Each box is one **beat**.

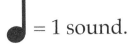 = 1 sound. 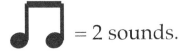 = 2 sounds.

Say the words and clap the **rhythm** while you stomp your feet to the **beat**.

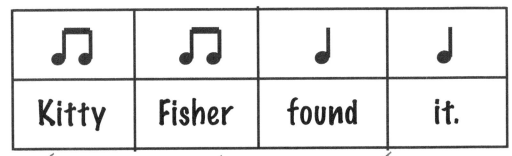

♫	♫	♫	♫
Lucy	Locket	lost her	pocket

♫	♫	♩	♩
Kitty	Fisher	found	it.

Draw the missing notes in the chart. Say and clap the rhythm. Then strum the rhythm on your ukulele.

Rain,	rain,	go a-	way.

Come a-	gain some	other	day.

Doggie, Doggie

Strum your ukulele to the beat as you sing.
Circle the bar lines.

American Folk Song

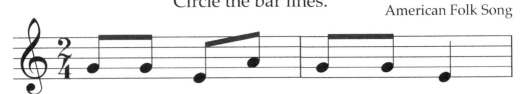

Dog - gie, dog - gie, where's your bone?

Some - one stole it   from your home.

♩ = 1 beat   ♫ = 1 beat

How many **beats** are in each **measure**?

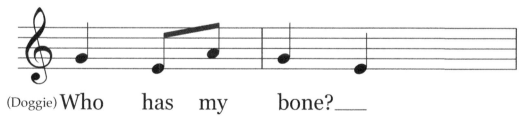

(Doggie) Who   has   my   bone?___

Copy the notes from the line above.

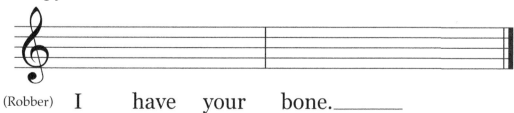

(Robber)   I   have   your   bone._____

Chapter 4

C and D

The 3rd string is C. It is between the G and E strings. C looks special because it gets its own line under the staff.

Draw 2 C's. Pluck C with your 1st (index) finger.

Create your own 8 beat pattern using G, C, E and A. Put one or two letters in each box. Then play your pattern.

Create another pattern. Which pattern do you like better? Why?

Ickle Ockle

Circle the C.

English Folk Song

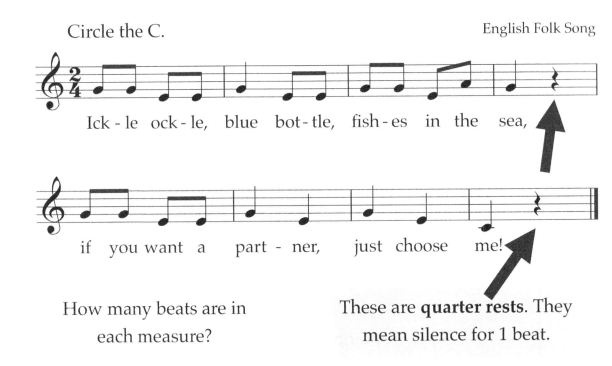

Ick - le ock - le, blue bot - tle, fish - es in the sea,

if you want a part - ner, just choose me!

How many beats are in
each measure?

These are **quarter rests**. They
mean silence for 1 beat.

Strum to the beat as you sing this song.
Strum up and down.

Old Mister Woodpecker

Circle the C.

How many rests can you find?

American Folk Song

Old Mis-ter Wood-peck-er tap-ping on a tree

Tap

Tap gently on wooden part of ukulele

Old Mis-ter Wood-peck-er tap it once a-gain

Tap

Tap again.

Old Mis-ter Wood-peck-er, that's the end!

Tap

Strum the rhythm.

Find something in the picture that has 2 sounds **(syllables)** like the word "city". Write the word here

_____ = ♫

Find something in the picture that has 1 sound **(syllable)** like the word "town". Write the word here.

_____ = ♩

Write your words in the chart.

Notes	♫	♩	♩	♩

Fill in the charts to create your own rhythm.

Notes				
Words				

Notes				
Words				

D hangs under the staff.
It touches the 1st line.
Draw 5 D's.

To play D, place your 1st finger on the C string in between the 1st and 2nd frets. Push down as you pluck the C string. How does the sound change?

Closet Key

The top number in the **time signature** tells us how many beats are in each measure.

African-American Song Game

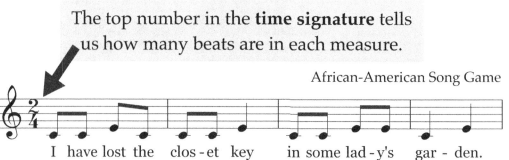

I have lost the clos-et key in some lad-y's gar - den.

5 Circle the D.

Help me find the clos-et key in some lad-y's gar - den.

How many hidden keys can you find in this book?

Create your own rhythm. Use ♩ or ♫ or 𝄽.

Agua de Limón

Circle the **time signature.**

Columbian Song Game

A - gua de li - món,   va - mos a ju - gar.

El que que - da so - lo   so - lo que - da - rá. ¡Jey!

Lemonade, let's play. The one who is
left alone will remain. Hey!

El Florón

Circle the D's.

Mexican Song Game

El   flo - rón   es - tá   en   la

ma - no   y̱ en   la   ma - no   el   flo -

A **half note** 𝅗𝅥 lasts for 2 beats.

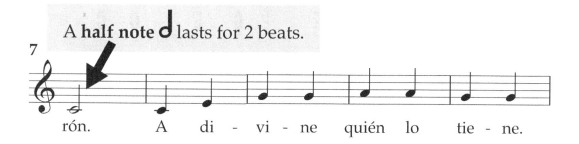

rón.   A   di - vi - ne   quién   lo   tie - ne.

O   se   que - da   de   plan - tón.

The flower is in the hand
And in the hand is the flower.
Guess who has it
Or it remains a seedling.

57

Say the tongue twister 5 times as fast as you can! Notice how there is a different string for each note. Play the notes on the ukulele.

Words	Six	swans	swam	swiftly.
Notes	♩	♩	♩	♫
Strings	G	A	G	E E

Words	Peter	picked	pepper	packets.
Notes	♫	♩	♫	♫
Strings	E G	E	G E	C C

Now create your own tongue twister. Use ♩ or ♫ words
from the list. Say your tongue twister. Play your new song.

Words				
Notes				
Letters				

♩

swans
swam
sleek
swift
six

♫

swiftly
southward
sweetly
swimming
sixty

Here is a tongue twister with its music on the staff.

Words	Peter	picked	pepper	packets.
Notes	♫	♩	♫	♫
Letters	E G	E	G E	C C

Pet - er   picked   pep - per   pack - ets.

Here's extra room to create 3 more tongue twister songs.

Words				
Notes				
Letters				

Words				
Notes				
Letters				

Words				
Notes				
Letters				

Write your 3 tongue twister songs on the staff. Add bar lines at the end of each line. Use these notes:

G   C   E   A

Rocky Mountain

Circle the **half notes.**

American Folk Song

Rock-y mount-ain, rock-y mount-ain, rock-y mount-ain high,

when you're on that rock-y mount-ain, hang your head and cry.

Stormy ocean, stormy ocean, stormy ocean
wide, when you're on that stormy ocean,
there's no place to hide.

Sunny valley, sunny valley, sunny valley low,
when you're in that sunny valley, sing it soft
and slow.

How many beats are in each measure?

Clap the rhythm while you stomp your feet to the beat.

Do,   do,   do,   do,   do   re - mem - ber   me.

Do,   do,   do,   do,   do   re - mem - ber   me.

What are some patterns that you notice in this music?
Which rhythms are the same? Which notes are the same?

Do the half notes ♩ share a pattern?

'Round and 'Round

Circle the half notes.

Caribbean Song Game

'Round   and   'round   we   must   go,

3

boom   ma - ka - le - li   chi   chi   boom.

If there is only one repeat sign, go
back to the beginning to repeat.

How many different ways can you
make a 4 beat rhythm?

5
Down   young   *(Kay - la)*   you   must   go,

7
boom   ma - ka - le - li   chi   chi   boom.

Sally Go 'Round the Sun

A **whole rest** 𝄻 means silence for the whole measure.

English Folk Song

A **dotted half note** 𝅗𝅥. lasts for 3 beats.

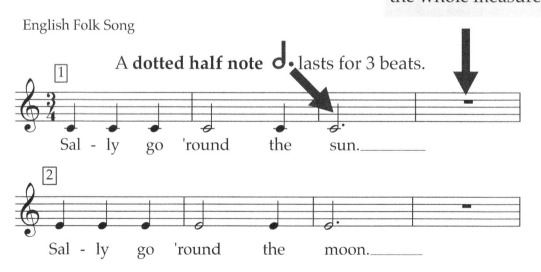

Sal - ly go 'round the sun._____

Sal - ly go 'round the moon._____

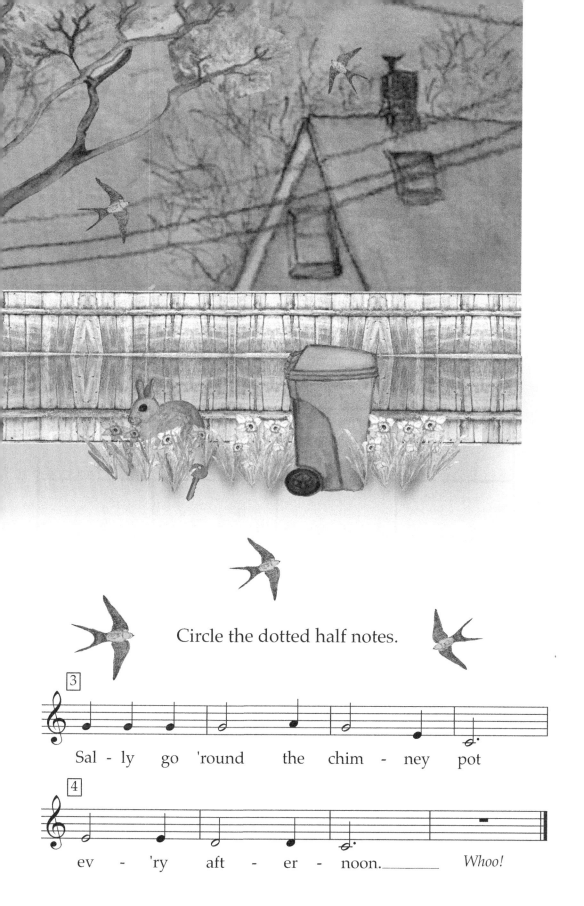

Circle the dotted half notes.

3
Sal - ly go 'round the chim - ney pot

4
ev - 'ry aft - er - noon._____ *Whoo!*

69

Use ♩ or ♫ or 𝄽 and C, D, E, G or A to create your own melody.

Notes				
Letters				

Notes				
Letters				

Write your melody on the staff.

Draw a bar line at the end of the measure.

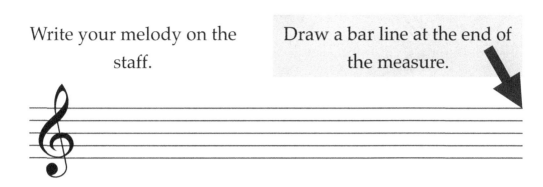

Gilly Gilly

American Folk Song

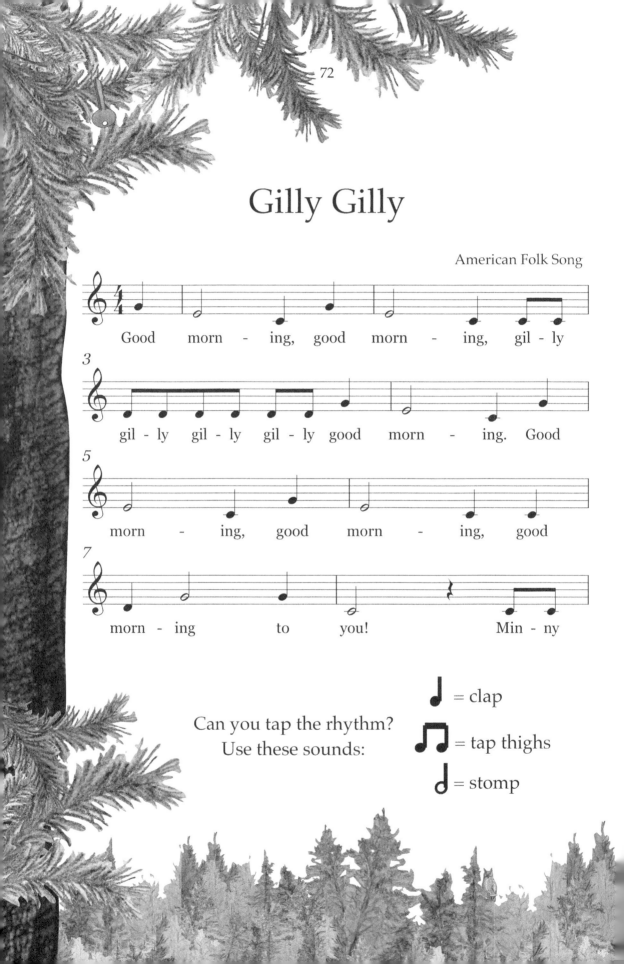

Good morn - ing, good morn - ing, gil - ly

gil - ly gil - ly gil - ly good morn - ing. Good

morn - ing, good morn - ing, good

morn - ing to you! Min - ny

♩ = clap

♫ = tap thighs

𝅗𝅥 = stomp

Can you tap the rhythm?
Use these sounds:

9
mack, min - ny mack, min - ny   min - ny min - ny mack, min - ny

11
mack, min - ny mack, min - ny   mo.   Min - ny

13
mack, min - ny mack, min - ny   min - ny min - ny mack, min - ny

15
mack,   min - ny   mack,   min - ny   mo.

Chapter 5
High C

To play High C, place your 2nd finger on the A string in between the 2nd and 3rd frets. Push down as you pluck the A string.

High C is in the 3rd space on the staff.

Draw 4 High C's.

What'll I Do with the Baby-o

Circle the High C.

Appalachian Folk Song

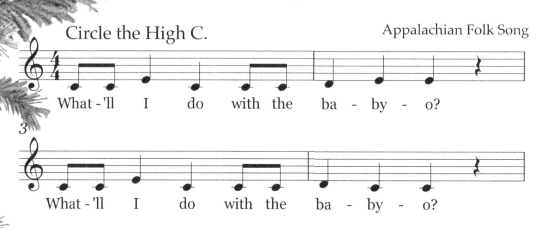

What - 'll   I   do   with the   ba - by - o?

What - 'll   I   do   with the   ba - by - o?

What - 'll   I   do   with the   ba - by - o   if

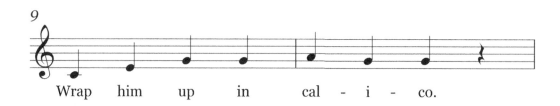

he   don't   go   to   sleep - y - o?

Wrap   him   up   in   cal - i - co.

11

Wrap   him   up   in   cal - i - co.

13

Wrap   him   up   in   cal - i - co.

15

Send   him   to   his   mam - my - o.

Funga Alafia

A **whole note** ◯ lasts for 4 beats.

Circle the whole notes.

West African Greeting Song

Fun - ga   a - la - fi - a,   a - shay,   a - shay.

5
Fun - ga   a - la - fi - a,   a - shay,   a - shay.

9
A - shay,   a - shay,   a - shay,   a - shay.

13
A - shay,   a - shay,   a - shay,   a - shay.

A **double bar line** means the song is over.

17
Fun - ga   a - la - fi - a,   a - shay,   a - shay.

Strum the beat   while you sing.

Use ♩ or ♫ or 𝄾 and C, D, E, G, A or High C to create your own melody. Then write your song on the staff.

Notes				
Letters				

Notes				
Letters				

Notes				
Letters				

Notes				
Letters				

C D E G A C

Put a double bar line at the end of your song.

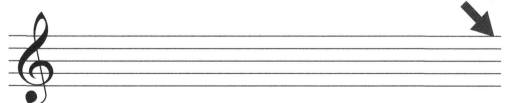

Bu Yu Ge

Stomp the quarter notes. Clap the eighth
notes. Touch your head when there is a rest.

Chinese Folk Song

Gi - ant   white waves, but I'm   not   a - fraid.

Hold - ing   up   the rud - der, row - ing   on.

Wa - ter,   home of   fish, I   cast   my   nets____

Cap-tur-ing a   big fish, laugh-ing, ha   ha   ha!

Dors, Dors

Sleep, sleep little baby. Here's mama's beautiful little
baby. If it's nice tomorrow, we'll visit Grandpa.

Acadian Lullaby

Dors, dors, le pe - tit bé - bé. C'est le beau p'tit

bé-bé à ma-man. Dors, dors, dors, dors, dors, dors, le bé-

bé à ma-man. de-main s'y fait beau j'i-rons au grand-père.

Dors,___ dors, le p'tit bé - bé. Dors, dors,

dors, dors, dors, dors, le bé - bé à ma-man.

Divide into 2 groups and play the rhythm: everyone stomps when
there is a half note. Group A stands up to clap eighth notes, but
sits down when Group B stands up to tap quarter notes. Group B
also sits down when Group A is clapping eighth notes.

Li'l Liza Jane

Clap the *Minny Mac* pattern with a
partner while you sing this song.

Countess Ada de Lachau

I got - ta house in Balt - i - more,

l'il Li - za Jane,

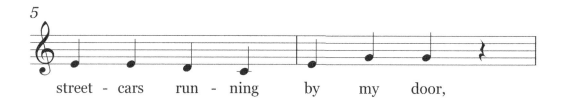

street - cars run - ning by my door,

l'il Li - za Jane.

Circle the High C's.

Oh, E - li - za,

l'il Li - za Jane.

Oh, E - li - za,

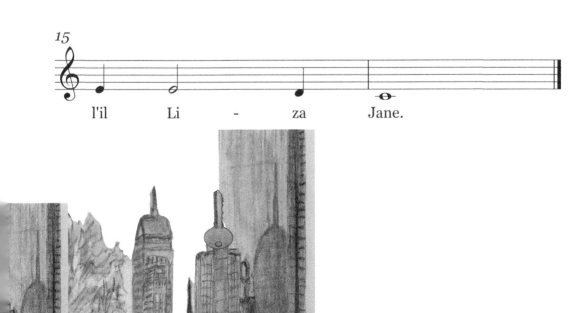

l'il Li - za Jane.

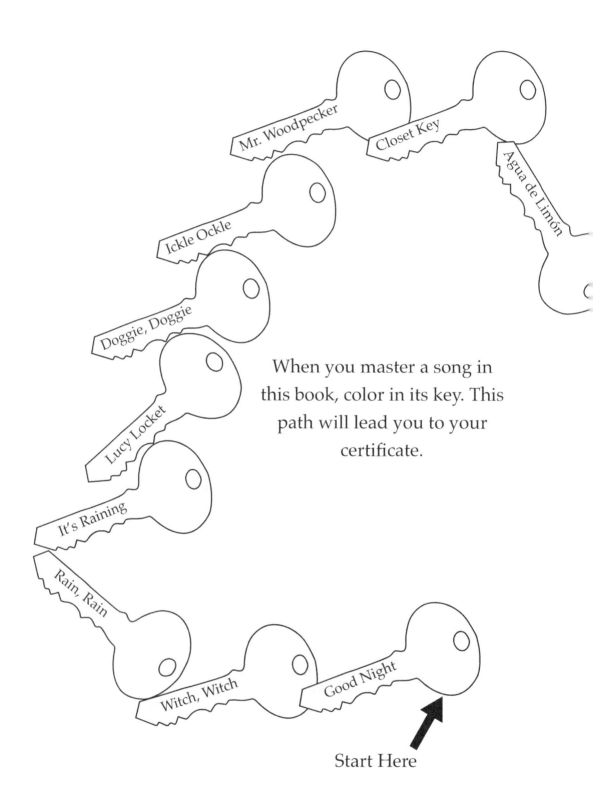

When you master a song in this book, color in its key. This path will lead you to your certificate.

Start Here

'Round and 'Round

Rocky Mountain

Sally Go 'Round

El Floron

Gilly, Gilly

Baby-O

Funga Alafia

Which song is your favorite?
Why?

Dors, Dors

Bu Yu Ge

Li'l Liza Jane

Bravo! Go to
page 97.

The Animals

red-shouldered hawk

house sparrow

common grackle

eastern cottontail rabbit

barn swallow

blackburnian warbler

great horned owl

plains zebra

downy woodpecker

domestic cat

herring gull

white-tailed deer

Canada goose

mute swan

domestic dog

snow bunting

mourning dove

American robin

northern cardinal

eastern chipmunk

northern mockingbird

eastern grey squirrel

Which animal in this book would you like as a pet? Why?

The Games

24. **Witch, Witch** is a chasing game. The Children gather in a large, open play area around one player who is the "Witch." At the end of the song, the Children scatter. The first child the Witch tags is the next Witch in a repetition of the game.

38. **Lucy Locket** is a chasing game. The players sit in a circle. One player, "Lucy," walks around the outside of the circle holding a bean bag. On the last note of the song, Lucy drops the bean bag behind the nearest seated player, who must pick up the bean bag, then chase Lucy in the same direction around the circle until Lucy sits down in the chaser's space. The chaser's challenge is to tag Lucy before she reaches his space.

42. **Doggie, Doggie** is a guessing game. One player stays with her back to the group, eyes closed. She is the Doggie. Another player is the Robber, who holds the Doggie's bone. The Doggie sings, "Who has my bone?" The Robber answers, "I have your bone." Keeping her eyes closed, the Doggie guesses who the Robber is.

46. **Ickle Ockle** is a choosing game. Players sit in a circle. One player, the Fisherman, stands in the center and points to one player per beat, going around the circle. The player the Fisherman points to on the word "me" wins.

52. **Closet Key** is an object hiding game. Children sit in a circle with their hands behind their backs. One child, the Finder, is sent out of the room while the teacher hands a key to one player. The Finder is called back into the room. All the children pretend to have the key behind their back as they sing. The Finder walks around the perimeter of the circle as the children give the Finder hints by singing gradually louder the closer the Finder is to the key, and gradually softer the further away from the key. The song is sung 3 times. Then the Finder has 3 chances to guess who has the key.

56. **El Florón** is a passing game. Children sit in a circle with their hands behind their backs. Everyone closes their eyes. One child is given an object (the "flower"). The children open their eyes and sing while the player with the flower discreetly passes it along to their neighbor, who in turn may pass it around the circle in either direction. The passing continues until the song is finished. Whoever guesses who has the flower at the end of the song wins the game.

57. In **Agua de Limón,** children hold hands in a circle and move clockwise as they sing. At the end of the song, a leader calls out a number such as "Two!" or "Three!" Students must scramble to form groups of either two or three. Whoever is left without a partner is the new leader.

66. '**Round and 'Round** is a moving circle game. A different player's name is called each time the song is sung. The chosen player must crouch down as he continues to move in the circle. The song is repeated until everyone in the circle is crouching.

68. **Sally Go 'Round the Sun** is a movement game. Join hands in a circle and step in time to the 1st beat of each measure as you move clockwise. When you say *Whoo*, let go of hands and jump in the opposite direction. Hold hands again and repeat the song, this time moving in a counterclockwise direction.

72. **Gilly Gilly** is a greeting game. Players sit in a circle. As everyone sings, one player marches around the inside of the circle. She stops in front of the closest seated player when "Good morning to you!" is sung. The chosen player stands up and both players clap "minny mack" like this: on beat 1 of each measure, players clap. On beat 3 of every measure, both players clap each others' hands. These two standing players separate when the song is repeated. They both march inside the circle while everyone sings the song again. Then they both find 2 new partners to play "minny mack." The song is repeated until everyone in the circle is standing.

Certificate of
Achievement

Congratulations to

_____

Student's Name

who has mastered all the music in

Ukulele! Level 1

and officially become a composer.

_____

Teacher's Signature

_____

Date

Made in the USA
Las Vegas, NV
07 December 2023

82268638R00057